IN FOCUS

BIG BEASTS

KINGFISHER
LONDON & NEW YORK

Copyright © Macmillan Publishers International Ltd 2018
Published in the United States by Kingfisher,
175 Fifth Ave., New York, NY 10010
Kingfisher is an imprint of Macmillan Children's Books, London
All rights reserved.

Distributed in the U.S. and Canada by Macmillan,
175 Fifth Ave., New York, NY 10010

Library of Congress Cataloging-in-Publication data has been applied for.

Series editor: Hayley Down
Designer: Jeni Child

ISBN (PB): 978-0-7534-7429-7
ISBN (HB): 978-0-7534-7428-0

Kingfisher books are available for special promotions and premiums.
For details contact: Special Markets Department, Macmillan,
175 Fifth Ave., New York, NY 10010.

For more information, please visit
www.kingfisherbooks.com

Printed in China

9 8 7 6 5 4 3 2 1

1TR/0418/WKT/UG/128GSM

Picture credits
The Publisher would like to thank the following for permission to reproduce their material.
Top = t; Bottom = b; Center = c; Left = l; Right = r
Cover: Getty/Theo Allofs; Back cover: iStock/seb_c_est_bien; cover flap: iStock/AndreAnita; Pages 1 Shutterstock/alesksander hunta;
3 iStock/JohnCarnemolla; 4–5 iStock/SKLA; 4t iStock/dottedhippo; 4b Shutterstock/Vaclav Sebek; 5t iStock/ntdanai; 5b Shutterstock/
Krzysztof Odziomek; 6 iStock/Janet K Scott; 7t iStock/wakila; 7c iStock/ShaneGross; 7b Getty/Ben Lascelles/Nature Picture Library;
8–9 Shutterstock/Johnathan Pledger; 10t Alamy/Stephen Frink Collection; 10c iStock/Freder; 10b Alamy/Nature Picture Library;
11tl iStock/Serjio74; 11tr iStock/Musat; 11c iStock/photomaru; 11b Getty/Robert Muckley; 12–13 iStock/dottedhippo; 13 Creative
Commons; 14 Alamy/Stocktrek Images; 15t Alamy/National Geographic Creative; 15c Alamy/Florilegius; 15b Science Photo Library;
16 (1) Alamy/Gary Roberts; 17 (2) Alamy/Natural History Museum; 17 (3) SPL/B.G Thomson; 17 (4) iStock/Kanawa_Studio;
17 (5) Shutterstock/Nimai; 17 (6) Shutterstock/reptiles4all; 17 (7) iStock/CraigRJD; 17 (8) Roman Uchytel; 17 (9) Alamy/Minden Pictures;
17 (10) SPL/Jaime Chririnos; 18–19 Shutterstock/Vaclav Sebek; 20tl iStock/Dimos_istock; 20tr Alamy/blickwinkel; 20bl Getty/Tier Und
Naturfotografie J und Sohns; 20br iStock/CraigRJD; 21t Alamy/National Geographic Creative; 21bl Shutterstock/Ondrek Prosicky;
21br Shutterstock/Audrey Snider-Bell; 22–23 Alamy/Cheryl Schneider; 23t iStock/Freder; 23b iStock/JohnPitcher; 24 (1) Alamy/
Cimages; 25 (2), (4), (6) & (9) iStock/reptiles4all; 25 (3) Shutterstock/Stuart G Porter; 25 (5) iStock/Snowleopard1; 25 (7) Alamy/
Mattijs Kuijpers; 25 (8) iStock/LenSoMy; 25 (10) SPL/Jaimie Chirinos; 26 iStock/Bobbushphoto; 27t Shutterstock/Dennis W Donohue;
27c iStock/JohnCarnemolla; 27b Alamy/Hemis; 28 Alamy/Minden Pictures; 29t iStock/SHAWSHANK61; 29b iStock/Christie85;
30–31 Alamy/Ron Niebrugge; 32tl iStock/fishcat007; 32tr Shutterstock/Volodymyr Brudiak; 32bl iStock/jez_bennett;
32br Shutterstock/Johnathan Pledger; 33tl Alamy/Richard Garvey-Williams; 33bl iStock/Photocech; 33br Alamy/Alissa Everett;
34–35 iStock/ntdanai; 36–37 iStock/Harry-Eggens; 36 iStock/Chilkoot; 38tl iStock/SerrNovik; 38tr iStock/JohnCarnemolla; 38bl iStock/
Gleb_Ivanov; 38br Getty/John White Photos; 39tr iStock/Ve_ro_sa; 39bl Alamy/imageBROKER; 39br Shutterstock/Meister Photos;
40–41 iStock/Byronsdad; 42 Alamy/F1online digitale Bildagentur GmbH; 43t iStock/KeithSzafranski; 43b Alamy/Minden Pictures;
44–45 Getty/Barcroft Media; 46t Getty/Carrie Vonderhaar/Ocean Futures Society; 46bl Alamy/WaterFrame; 46br iStock/ystudio;
47t Getty/ullstein bild; 47bl Creative Commons; 47br Alamy/Minden Pictures; 48–49 Getty/Mauricio Handler; 48 iStock/
EXTREMEPHOTOGRAPHER; 50–51 iStock/ShaneGross; 51t Alamy/imageBROKER; 51b Getty/Flip Nicklin/Minden Pictures;
52–53 Superstock/Cultura Limited; 54 & 55t Alamy/Scubazoo; 55c Alamy/National Geographic Creative; 55b iStock/MelanieMaya;
56–57 Getty/Prisma by Dukas; 58 Shutterstock/Krzystof Odiomek; 59t Shutterstock/wildestanimal; 59b Alamy/BIOSPHOTO; 60 iStock/
Anagramm; 61 iStock/DavidFettesPhotography; 62 Alamy/Paulette Sinclair; 63 iStock/BraunS.

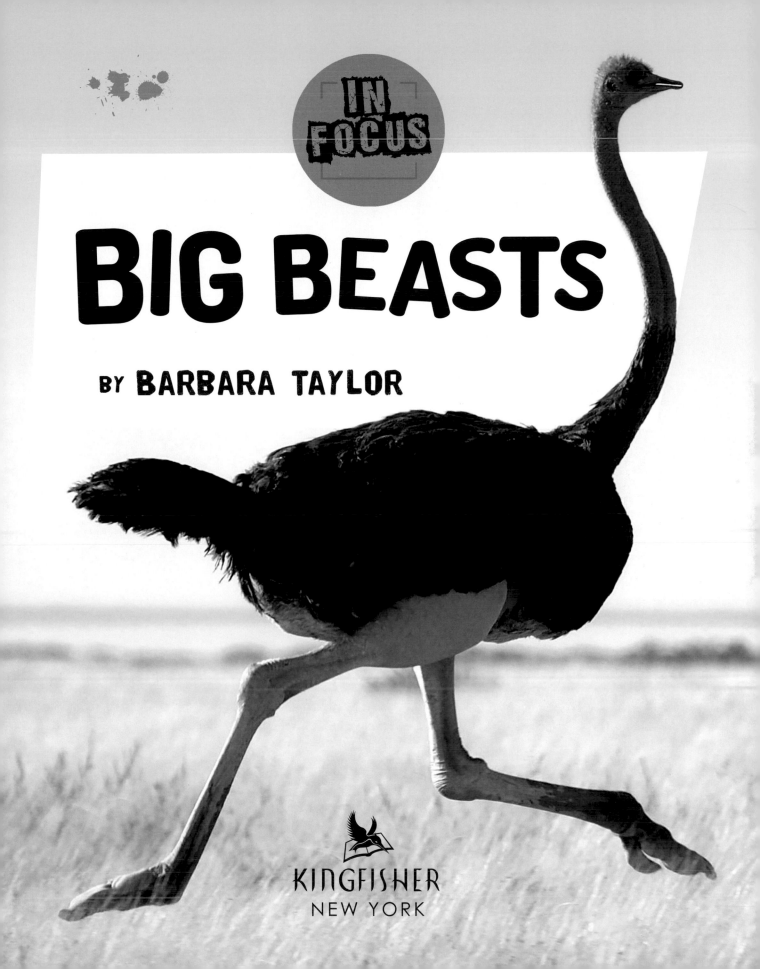

IN FOCUS

BIG BEASTS

BY **BARBARA TAYLOR**

KINGFISHER
NEW YORK

CONTENTS

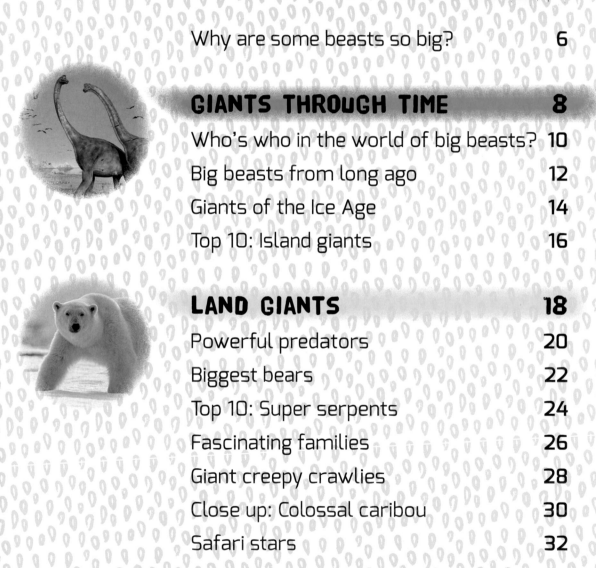

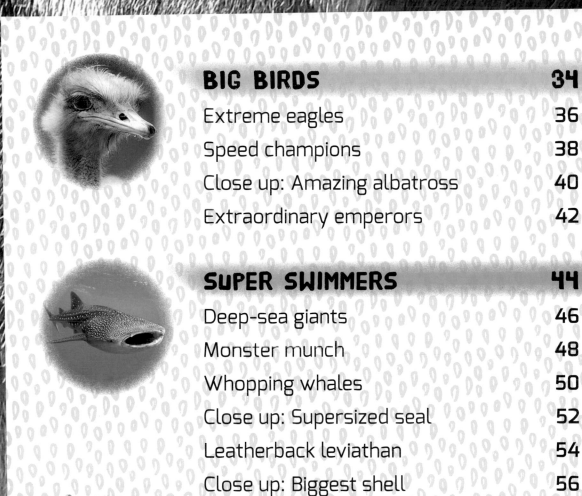

WHY ARE SOME BEASTS SO BIG?

Our planet is home to some truly enormous beasts: gigantic whales, enormous elephants, and bears so big they tower over a human. Surprisingly, the biggest beasts of all time are not the **dinosaurs** but today's whales. The water supports their heavy body, making it possible for a blue whale to weigh three times more than a dinosaur of the same size.

Back on dry land, the biggest beasts usually eat a lot of food and live for a long time. Many big beasts, such as the saltwater crocodile, become giants because they grow slowly and continue growing throughout their life. The huge size of saltwater crocodiles makes them powerful **predators**, and many other predators, such as tigers or eagles, also use their large size to overcome their **prey**.

saltwater crocodile

INSIDE YOU'LL FIND . . .

. . . mammoth mammals

Imagine an animal nine times heavier than a cow. Male **AFRICAN ELEPHANTS** are this size, and they are the biggest beasts to walk on land today. An adult elephant's size makes it hard for predators to kill, so it is rarely attacked.

. . . ocean giants

The big beast that breaks all the records is the amazing **BLUE WHALE**. It grows to be longer than a basketball court and is the biggest animal the world has ever seen. Baby blue whales are 700 times heavier than a human baby at birth.

. . . bulky birds

If flying animals reached the massive sizes of big land or sea beasts, they would be too heavy to fly. Even so, the biggest eagles, such as **HARPY EAGLES**, are strong enough to catch and carry monkeys in their huge talons.

GIANTS THROUGH TIME

MAMMALS

Mammoth **mammals** range from giraffes, elephants, and orangutans on land to whopping whales and roly-poly seals in the oceans. There are even giant flying mammals, such as fruit bats with a **wingspan** of nearly 6.5 ft (2 m)! The unique feature of mammals is that female mammals feed their young on their milk. Mammals often have fur or hair.

orangutan

FISH

Many of the biggest fish are sharks, including the largest fish of them all: the whale shark, which is as long as two buses! Other super-sized sharks include the basking shark, which has a mouth that measures 3 ft (1 m) wide. Fish have an internal **skeleton** and **gills** to take in oxygen from the water.

basking shark

OF BIG BEASTS?

From mammals and **reptiles** to fish and bugs, big beasts occur in lots of animal groups. Their habitats are shrinking and this threatens the survival of the world's spectacular giant creatures.

REPTILES

Reptiles breathe air and have a scaly skin and a bony internal skeleton. The largest reptiles include giant tortoises as heavy as three men and snakes longer than a bus. Komodo dragons are also extremely large and fierce reptiles, which eat anything they can swallow and are strong enough to kill a human.

Komodo dragon

BIRDS AND BUGS

The size of bugs is limited by their external skeleton and their breathing system. Some bugs, however, do reach very large sizes, including the giant African snail, which lives for up to 10 years. Like bugs, most birds cannot grow too big, otherwise they would become too heavy to fly. Flightless birds, such as the super-speedy ostrich, however, can grow to enormous sizes!

giant snail

BIG BEASTS FROM LONG AGO

Your questions about dinosaurs and other ancient giant beasts answered!

Brachiosaurus

Which flying reptile was as big as a jet plane?

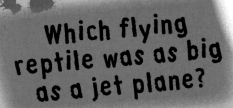

A flying reptile called *Quetzalcoatlus* was probably the largest flying animal of all time. It was a kind of **pterosaur**, which may have been related to the dinosaurs. With a wingspan of about 36 ft (11 m), this giant pterosaur was as tall as a giraffe when standing upright. It may have used prehistoric slopes as runways to gather enough speed and power to take off.

Which were the biggest dinosaurs?

The largest creatures ever to walk on land were the long-necked, plant-eating dinosaurs that were widespread about 150 million years ago. Giant dinosaurs are being discovered all the time. In 2017, the **fossilized** remains of *Patagotitan mayorum* were unearthed in Argentina. It weighed as much as 12 African elephants! Another super-massive dinosaur nicknamed "Dread" spent most of its life eating. Its stomach was about the size of a horse!

Which pouched mammal was as big as a rhino?

The giant wombat, *Diprotodon*, was the largest pouched animal that ever existed. It grew as big as a modern-day rhinoceros. Living in Australia some 300,000 years ago, the adult giant wombat was big enough to survive attacks by pouched lions. Baby giant wombats, however, would have been vulnerable to attack by giant monitor lizards and huge crocodiles that lived in Australia at this time.

Which ancient shark could bite a whale in half?

The largest predator on Earth, *Megalodon*, was a gigantic shark with a bite 6–10 times more powerful than that of today's great white shark. It ate whales and other large ocean mammals, such as sea cows and sea lions. Some of its big, jagged teeth (shown in this museum picture below) were nearly 7 in (20 cm) long, incredible when compared to the 2-in- (7-cm-) long teeth of today's biggest shark: the great white!

GIANTS OF THE ICE AGE

Ice Age

During the last Ice Age, which ended about 10,000 years ago, giant mammals roamed Earth. These Ice Age giants included woolly **mammoths** and woolly rhinos, giant ground sloths, giant elks, enormous cave bears, hyenas, and lions. In the Americas, there were even giant beavers the size of a black bear and armadillos as big as a small car!

We know about these Ice Age giants from fossils, cave paintings, and even frozen remains preserved in the ice in a similar way to Egyptian mummies. Being big may have helped these animals to compete for scarce resources and keep warm. These oversized animals became **extinct** at the end of the Ice Age because of climate change and hunting.

giant armadillo

The **GIANT ARMADILLOS** that roamed South America looked like their modern relatives, only they were much, much bigger! Their armored shell helped protect their soft belly and was so big that early humans used the empty shells as houses to find shelter from the snow.

As you would expect, the biggest deer ever to have lived, the **GIANT ELK**, also had the biggest antlers! Each antler was as long as a person and weighed as much as a suitcase—imagine holding two full suitcases on your head! The males used their massive antlers to impress females and intimidate rivals.

giant elk

giant sloth

GIANT GROUND SLOTHS were too big to live in trees. They reared up on their back legs and used their claws to strip leaves and twigs to eat, and to dig burrows.

ISLAND GIANTS

Isolated islands are the perfect habitats for unique species to evolve—just like these giant animals from past to present!

1 Coconut crab

It's hard to imagine a crab that weighs as much as a cat, but coconut crabs really are this heavy! They come out at night to rip open coconuts with their strong pincers. These giant crabs also eat meat and sometimes add rats, chickens, and smaller crabs to their diet.

2

Dead as a dodo

Gigantic flightless pigeons, called dodos, once lived on the island of Mauritius in the Indian Ocean.

3

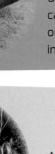

Giant rat

A giant rat is the stuff of nightmares! The Flores giant rat is over 3 ft (1 m) long, if you include its tail!

4

Komodo dragon

The largest, heaviest lizards in the world live on Indonesian islands where they are the only big predator.

5

Weta

Enormous flightless crickets as long as carrots inhabit the islands of New Zealand. They have survived since dinosaur times.

6

Super skink

The Solomon Islands skink reaches lengths of nearly 30 in (75 cm). Its tail grips branches like a monkey's tail.

7

Giant tortoise

The world's largest tortoises live on the Galápagos Islands and the Seychelles. They had no natural predators until people hunted them almost to extinction.

8

Giant rabbit

A **prehistoric** rabbit, called *Nuralagus*, weighed up to 12 times more than the heaviest modern rabbit!

9

Giant parrot

The kakapo is the world's heaviest parrot, weighing as much as a newborn baby! It is also the only parrot that cannot fly, but it can run very fast.

10

Elephant bird

Giant flightless elephant birds lived on Madagascar until about 1000 years ago. Some grew as heavy as half a ton—but not quite elephant sized!

Which island giant is your number one?

LAND GIANTS

POWERFUL

KILLER CATS

Big cats, such as tigers, lions, leopards, and jaguars, are expert hunters, using their size as well as their powerful teeth, jaws, and claws to overcome their prey. The biggest cat of all is the Siberian tiger—males can be up to 8.6 ft (2.6 m) long and jump as far as 30 ft (9 m).

Siberian tiger

LETHAL LIZARDS

Australia's largest lizard—and the second-largest lizard in the world—is the perentie. This fierce lizard can run as fast as an Olympic sprinter to catch speedy prey, such as rabbits. The perentie then shakes its prey violently until the animal dies.

perentie

PREDATORS

The biggest and scariest land predators are those with the strength and **stamina** to catch and kill their prey on their own. They include tigers, bears, eagles, snakes, lizards, and even gigantic spiders.

SKY HUNTERS

Did you know there is an owl as big as a small child flying through the snowy forests of Russia and Japan? With a wingspan of up to 6.5 ft (2 m), Blakiston's fish owl specializes in catching frogs and fish, sometimes killing salmon and trout up to three times as heavy as itself.

Blakiston's fish owl

SCARY SPIDERS

Some spiders would only just fit on your dinner plate—a scary thought! The Goliath tarantula is big enough to eat birds and is very aggressive, but its **venom** (luckily) is not strong enough to kill people. The Australian giant huntsman usually tries to run away rather than bite people, sometimes scampering across car dashboards.

Goliath tarantula

BIGGEST BEARS

Your questions about the world's biggest bears answered.

Do big bears have big cubs?

Surprisingly, massive mother bears are pregnant for a short time and give birth to tiny helpless cubs, which are only about the size of rats or guinea pigs. The cubs are born while the mothers are **hibernating** in a winter den. They have plenty of time to drink their mother's rich milk and grow big and strong before they emerge into the spring sunshine.

Which bear has the longest tongue?

Sun bears are only the size of big dogs, but their tongue is up to 10 in (25 cm) long! They climb into trees and lick up the honey from bees' nests with their extra-long tongue. This extended tongue also helps them find bugs hiding deep inside the holes and **crevices** in trees.

giant panda

Which are the biggest bears alive today?

The biggest bears are polar bears and the brown bears living on Kodiak Island, Alaska. Each of these immense bears can weigh as much as a small car. The polar bear is the tallest bear—the biggest one measured so far stood 11 ft (3.4 m) when upright on its back legs. That's about the same height as two tall people standing one on top of the other!

TOP 10 SUPER SERPENTS

Which are the biggest snakes on the planet?

1 Huge and heavy

The world's heaviest snake today is the anaconda (above), which weighs about the same as five children. It lives in the rivers of the Amazon rain forest.

2 Australian record-breaker

The biggest non-venomous snake in Australia is the amethystine. This 28-ft- (8.5-m-) long snake hunts at night for small mammals, birds, bats, and rats.

3 Fastest giant

The athletic black mamba can move faster than most people can run! This giant snake grows over 13 ft (4 m) and is the longest venomous snake in Africa.

4 Most dangerous

The taipan is the largest venomous snake in the world. Its venom is powerful enough to kill 100 people with just one bite!

7 Asian giant

The Indian python of South Asia grows up to 20 ft (6.4 m) long. This python can climb trees and swim.

8 Hooded king

The king cobra is the longest venomous snake in the world, reaching over 18 ft (5.5 m) long. The venom from a king cobra is strong enough to kill an elephant!

9 Longest fangs

The gaboon viper has the longest **fangs** of any snake. Its long, hollow curved teeth are up to 2 in (5 cm) long and deliver large amounts of venom when the snake bites.

5 Longest body

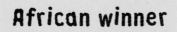

Growing up to 30 ft (9 m) long, the reticulated python is the world's longest snake. It can eat animals as large as deer or pigs.

10 Ultimate champion

The biggest, longest, and heaviest snake ever found is called *Titanoboa*. This prehistoric snake was big enough to eat crocodiles.

6 African winner

The African rock python is Africa's biggest snake. Its 25-ft- (7.5-metre-) long body coils around an antelope or crocodile and squeezes it to death.

Which super serpent is your number one?

FASCINATING FAMILIES

The male and female animals of the same species can vary in size. Males are often bigger than females if they have to fight rival males to win females for **mating**. Male deer, elephants, and frogs are bigger than the females for this reason. For animals that live in groups, such as lions, the males defend the group. Big males are better at driving away enemies to keep their group safe.

However, it's often an advantage for females to be bigger than their mates. The large size of female spiders, snakes, or birds of prey allows them to have bigger babies (or more babies) or lay bigger eggs (or more eggs). Big females can also compete for scarce resources more easily. Some female birds of prey are up to twice as heavy as the males.

bighorn sheep

male lion with cubs

MALE LIONS defend a group, called a pride, of females and their cubs. They fight off other males who try to mate with their females and also protect the cubs from predators. The long, shaggy mane of a male lion makes him look bigger and more dangerous and also protects his neck in a fight.

female elephant and calf

FEMALE ELEPHANTS are pregnant for nearly two years and give birth to very big babies, called calves. They usually have just one calf at a time, which can stand up within an hour of its birth. A newborn elephant weighs more than the average adult human! It feeds on its mother's nourishing milk for up to six years.

ostrich and eggs

The biggest birds in the world also lay the biggest eggs. The **OSTRICH** lays the biggest egg of all the birds alive today. It is equal in volume to 24 chickens' eggs, and the shell is so strong that a person can stand on the egg without breaking the shell.

The male African **GOLIATH BEETLE** weighs nearly as much as an apple and is probably the heaviest insect. This beetle flies well, but if it grew any bigger, it would be too heavy to fly.

GIANT CREEPY CRAWLIES

From beastly beetles to massive millipedes, creepy crawlies come in bigger sizes than you might imagine!

Is it a twig? Is it a pipe? No—it has legs! It's a **GIANT STICK INSECT**. It is the longest insect in the world and would fit across two pages of this book.

Caterpillars of the **HERCULES MOTH** grow up to 7 in (17 cm) long and would only just fit on an adult's hand. Once they hatch from their chrysalis after the caterpillar stage, moths do not grow any larger.

The **SAINT HELENA EARWIG** is definitely too big to fit inside your ear! Some have reached lengths of nearly 4 in (10 cm), but sadly this giant creepy crawly is probably extinct.

The giant South African **PILL MILLIPEDE** rolls up into a ball as big as a ping-pong ball when it is threatened. The armor-like plates on the top of its body fit together to make a protective case thst hides its soft belly.

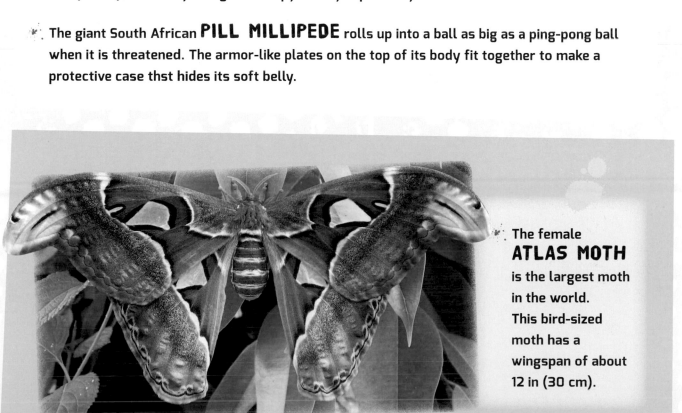

The female **ATLAS MOTH** is the largest moth in the world. This bird-sized moth has a wingspan of about 12 in (30 cm).

COLOSSAL CARIBOU

Caribou, or reindeer, are the only deer species in which both males and females have antlers. These enormous deer can eat up to 13 lb (6 kg) of food a day after their long annual **migrations**. Caribou have large hooves to carry their weight over snow. Each hoof has a hollow space underneath—a bit like a spoon—to help the deer dig through the snow, while hard edges help the deer to grip on icy ground.

More about caribou

Height (to shoulder): 4–5 ft (1.2–1.5 m)
Weight: 220–500 lb (100–227 kg)
Food: plants—especially grasses
Home: Asia, Europe, Greenland, North America

SAFARI

ENORMOUS ELEPHANTS

With ears the size of tablecloths and the longest nose of any living animal, the African elephant breaks all kinds of records. Males grow through most of their long life. They reach ages of over 70 years and may be twice as heavy as females. A large elephant weighs as much as 80 people!

African elephant

REMARKABLE RHINOS

The largest of the five species of rhinoceros is the white rhino. It is the second-largest land animal, after the elephant, and weighs as much as a large truck! The white rhino has a wide, square top lip that helps it munch through lots of grass each day, like a living lawn mower.

white rhino

STARS

The three biggest land animals are the elephant, the rhinoceros, and the hippopotamus. These vast vegetarians have to munch a lot of plants to keep their beastly body working.

HUGE HIPPOS

In third place is the barrel-shaped hippopotamus. This hefty animal spends six hours a night eating grass. It is dangerous and aggressive, able to charge at speeds of up to 20 mph (30 kph) on land if it is threatened. During the day, it relaxes in rivers, pools, or mud holes and can hold its breath underwater for up to 30 minutes.

hippos

HORNS AND TUSKS

Poachers hunt elephants and hippos for their valuable ivory tusks and teeth. Rhinos are killed for their huge horns, which are used to make dagger handles or ground up for traditional Chinese medicine. These mega-mammals all face a difficult future and may soon become extinct in the wild.

tusks

BIG BIRDS

EXTREME EAGLES

Which eagles are the biggest and most powerful beasts? Your questions answered.

Which eagle's nest weighs as much as a 4x4 car?

Eagle parents add to their stick nest, or eyrie, every year so the nest grows to an enormous size. Some nests contain 400 or more large branches and are so heavy they eventually come crashing down to the ground. The biggest eagle's nest ever recorded belonged to a pair of bald eagles. It was 9.5 ft (3 m) wide, 20 ft (6 m) deep, and weighed up to 3 tons, which is as much as an army jeep! Golden eagles also build huge nests—the biggest recorded nest was nearly 16 ft (5 m) deep!

Which is the biggest eagle in the world?

The Steller's sea eagle is the heaviest known eagle and the largest of all the sea eagles—even more powerful than a bald eagle! These rare Siberian eagles have excellent eyesight and may swoop down more than 99 ft (30 m) from the sky to catch fish, such as salmon. They drive their huge, razor-sharp talons into their prey and don't let go until it is dead.

Steller's sea eagle

Which ancient eagle was the "tiger" of New Zealand?

The largest eagle of all time, the Haast's eagle, was like a tiger because it was a top predator and had claws as big as a tiger's claws. These giant birds were about twice the weight of a golden eagle. They preyed on huge flightless birds called moas and became extinct about 500 years ago, soon after the moas died out. Haast's eagles struck their prey at speeds of 50 mph (80 kph), delivering a crushing blow to the head and neck with their terrible talons.

SPEED

OSTRICH

As tall as a soccer goalpost and weighing up to 22 st (145 kg), the African ostrich is the largest and heaviest bird alive today. It also has the biggest eyes of any land animal—they are an incredible 2 in (5 cm) in diameter. The ostrich is the only bird with two toes on each foot, which help it to sprint at up to 44 mph (70 kph). This makes an ostrich the second-fastest runner.

run, ostrich, run!

EMU

The second-largest bird in the world, the Australian emu, stands up to 6.5 ft (2 m) tall and weighs over 9.5 st (60 kg). Emus would make good marathon runners. They can jog at speeds of 4.5 mph (7 kph) over the vast outback to search for food and water, but they are also capable of a sprint finish at speeds of up to 30 mph (48 kph)!

enormous emu

CHAMPIONS

The biggest birds in the world—ostriches, emus, cassowaries, and rheas—are too heavy to fly. But they are very good at running fast on their long, powerful legs.

RHEA

Flocks of rheas roam the South American grasslands, running at up to 40 mph (64 kph) on their long, strong legs. Their wings are useless for flying but handy for balancing or changing direction when the rheas run fast. Rheas are the smallest of the big flightless birds, but still grow 5 ft (1.5 m) tall and weigh up to 4 st (25 kg).

rapid rhea

CASSOWARY

A fierce rain forest giant, the Australian cassowary has claws up to 5 in (12 cm) long on each foot. It uses these claws for defense; not for catching prey, since its diet mainly consists of fruit and berries. No one is sure why the cassowary has a strange helmet on its head. It may help the bird push through the rain forest, or attract a mate, or even amplify the cassowary's booming calls.

defense down under!

CLOSE UP

AMAZING ALBATROSS

The biggest seabirds of all, wandering albatrosses, also have the largest wingspan of any bird. They spend most of their life gliding effortlessly over the Southern Ocean on their extra-long outstretched wings. These amazing birds may travel hundreds of miles in a day—just imagine flying 100 miles to find breakfast. They feed at the surface of the ocean at night, using their powerful, hooked bill to grab prey. Wandering albatrosses can eat up to 6 lb (3 kg) of food at one sitting and are sometimes too heavy to take off after a really big meal.

More about wandering albatrosses

Average size: wingspan over 10 ft (3 m); average weight 1–2 st (6.5–12 kg)

Average lifespan: over 60 years

Food: fish, squid, cuttlefish, crustaceans, and dead seals and penguins

Big fact: Albatrosses raise only one chick every two years. The chick stays in the nest for about nine months. When it is fully grown, the chick is heavier than its parents!

EXTRAORDINARY EMPERORS

Discover incredible facts about the biggest penguins of them all—the extraordinary emperor penguin!

EMPEROR PENGUINS grow up to 4 ft (1.1 m) tall—the height of a six-year-old child—and weigh 20 times more than the smallest penguin, the little penguin!

Living in **ANTARCTICA**, the coldest place on Earth, emperor penguins are experts at keeping warm. Their tightly packed feathers are coated in oil to make them waterproof and keep out the freezing seawater.

Thick layers of **FATTY BLUBBER** under the skin also help keep emperor penguins warm. These enormous penguins huddle together for warmth, which is unusual as most penguins like to keep a safe distance from each other!

Male emperor penguins keep their egg warm for 60 days by holding it against a warm patch of skin called a brood pouch. This is called **INCUBATING** the egg. The males do not eat during incubation and may lose as much as half their body weight.

Without the warmth of the parents' **BROOD POUCH**, the emperor penguin's eggs and chicks would die in a few minutes on the freezing cold Antarctic ice.

Emperor penguins breed on **SEA ICE** so they are the only birds that never set foot on land!

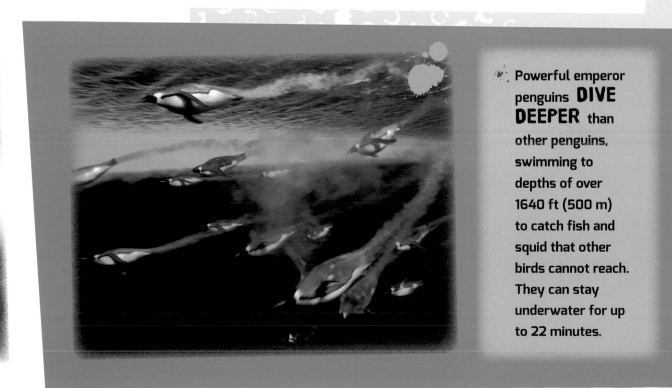

Powerful emperor penguins **DIVE DEEPER** than other penguins, swimming to depths of over 1640 ft (500 m) to catch fish and squid that other birds cannot reach. They can stay underwater for up to 22 minutes.

SUPER SWIMMERS

DEEP-SEA

GIANT SQUID

Lurking in the ocean depths are the world's largest **invertebrates**. The giant squid is about 36 ft (11 m) long and has eyes as big as dinner plates. The colossal squid is even bigger, perhaps 45 ft (14 m) or more in length. It has nasty hooks as well as suckers on its tentacles, which it uses to fight sperm whales that dive down from the surface for a succulent squid snack.

LEGGY CRAB

Looking like a massive underwater spider, the Japanese spider crab has a legspan of over 13 ft (4 m), which is twice as long as an average bed! It moves slowly over the ocean floor on its 10 long legs, searching for dead bodies to eat, or feeding on shellfish and worms. The leggy crab is protected by its hard shell, and it decorates this shell with sea creatures for **camouflage**.

Humboldt squid

Japanese spider crab

GIANTS

In the depths of the oceans, the water is inky black and freezing cold. Yet some of the ocean's largest animals thrive in these challenging conditions.

TERRIFIC TUBE WORMS

Giant tube worms over 6.5 ft (2 m) long live up to 8500 ft (2600 m) below the ocean waves in places where superheated water gushes out of the ocean floor. They live inside a long narrow tube and use a red "plume" to take in gases and minerals from the water. **Bacteria** living inside the worm's body make food for the worm from the minerals and, in return, have a safe place to live.

tube worms

INCREDIBLE ISOPOD

Did you know that the deep ocean is home to giant relatives of the tiny wood lice that live on land? The giant isopod works slowly and, to save energy, it doesn't move around very much. This incredible isopod eats mostly dead animals that drift down from above. It eats as much as possible at one time so it can survive for years without eating again!

isopod

MONSTER MUNCH

How do the ocean's biggest predators catch their prey? Your questions answered.

Which jellyfish looks like a lion?

The lion's mane jellyfish is named after its mane of long, hairlike tentacles. The 197-ft- (60-m-) long tentacles make this jellyfish one of the longest animals in the world—as well as the largest jellyfish! Armed with millions of stings, the tentacles trap and kill fish, and even other jellyfish.

Why can a great white shark take such big bites?

A great white shark's mouth has loose-fitting jaws, which slide forward to open very wide. It only takes a few seconds for the jaws to move, allowing the shark to take big bites in a flash. In every bite, a great white shark uses about 80 teeth. If any break off, they are replaced by new teeth growing underneath. This shark may use up to 30,000 teeth in a lifetime!

How does a great hammerhead shark catch a stingray?

Stingrays are a favorite food of the great hammerhead shark. They bury themselves in the sand on the seabed to hide from predators. However, the shark can detect the electrical pulses given off by a hidden stingray. It pins the fish down with its "hammer" and takes bites out of its winglike fins until it is dead.

Pacific octopus

How many suckers does a giant Pacific octopus have?

This smart, sneaky octopus has up to 2240 suckers on its eight long arms. If you could put one of these octopuses next to a giraffe, it would be at least as tall, perhaps even taller! Yet this giant octopus hatches out from an egg the size of a grain of rice. Upon hatching, each one of the tiny arms of the baby octopus has 14 suckers!

The largest whale with teeth, the **SPERM WHALE**, also has the biggest brain of any animal alive today. A sperm whale's brain weighs almost 20 lbs (9 kg) and is more than five times heavier than a human brain!

WHOPPING WHALES

Which whales break all the records?

Reaching lengths of 88.5 ft (27 m), the **FIN WHALE** is the second-longest whale. One adult can weigh as much as 10 large elephants!

Named after their enormous bow-shaped jaws, **BOWHEAD WHALES** eat huge amounts of **plankton** in every gulp. They live in cold Arctic oceans and have the thickest fatty **blubber** of all the whales (19 in / 48 cm), which keeps them warm.

The **HUMPBACK WHALE** holds the record for having the longest flippers – 16 ft (5 m) long! On their migrations, these whales may travel as far as 16,000 mi (25,750 km) in search of food and warm places to have their young.

The massive head of a **RIGHT WHALE** makes up a third of its total body length (up to 60 ft / 18 m). Hanging from each side of its giant jaws are 200 fringed plates, which filter plankton and small fish from the water.

Giant **BLUE WHALES** are over 98 ft (30 m) long. They can make sounds louder than a jet engine to communicate with other whales up to 994 mi (1600 km) away. They probably live for up to 100 years.

CLOSE UP

SUPERSIZED SEAL

The southern elephant seal is not only the largest of the seals; it is the world's largest meat-eating animal. Males can weigh up to eight times more than females. These chunky seals live in Antarctic oceans rich in food—their favorite is squid—and can dive to depths of more than 1 mile (1.6 km) in search of a meal. The name of this seal comes from its trunk-like nose, which amplifies its bellowing calls. Loud noises help males keep their rivals at a safe distance so they can mate with as many females as possible.

More about elephant seals

Male size: length up to 20 ft (6 m); weight up to 4.5 tons

Food: mainly squid, also fish and crustaceans (shrimplike creatures)

Lifespan: 20–22 years

Big fact: The milk that southern elephant seal mothers feed their pups contains over 50 percent fat! The pups grow fast on this rich diet, and after one month they weigh four times their birth weight.

LEATHERBACK LEVIATHAN

The leatherback turtle is the largest of all the turtles and one of the largest reptiles on Earth. This turtle is as long as a tall person and the biggest ones weigh more than 11 men! Leatherback turtles swim faster, dive deeper, and travel farther than other sea turtles. They are named after their dark-blue, rubbery skin, which looks like leather. This strange skin helps the turtle to make deep dives, because it can be squashed by the huge pressure of the water—a hard shell would crack and break.

BEASTLY FACT

Few **PREDATORS** are able to tackle leatherbacks because of their huge size, but great white sharks and orcas sometimes eat them. Leatherback turtles can swim in colder oceans than other turtles because their large body size, dark color, thick layers of body fat, and clever blood system help them stay warmer than the surrounding water. This means they can still keep themselves warm even when the water they are swimming through is almost freezing.

leatherback

four flippers

Leatherback turtles have front **FLIPPERS** that are almost 10 ft (3 m) long. They use these powerful flippers like wings to swim up to 21 mph (35 kph). Leatherbacks can dive to depths of 4000 ft (1200 m).

BEASTLY ★ FACT

It's hard to believe, but the leatherback's giant body is fueled by a diet of **JELLYFISH!** They have hundreds of spines in their mouth and throat to trap and tear up their slippery, gooey prey. Jellies are easy to catch, and the leatherback eats a lot of them at once, including the enormous lion's mane jellyfish!

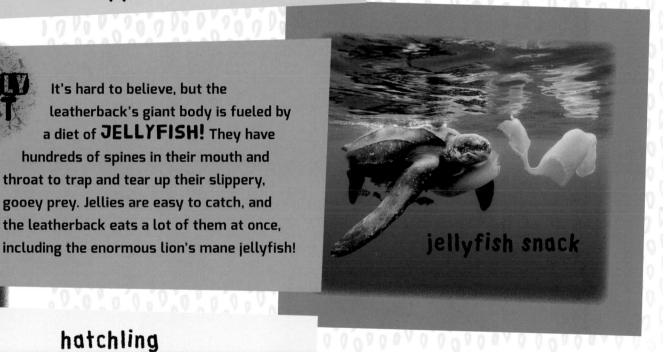

jellyfish snack

hatchling

Female leatherback turtles lay 80–100 **EGGS** in one clutch and lay eight or nine clutches in each breeding season. They dig a hole with their flippers in a sandy beach, lay their eggs, and then return to the sea. The eggs and baby turtles are left to fend for themselves.

BEASTLY ★ FACT

BIGGEST SHELL

The giant clam is the world's biggest shellfish. It weighs as much as two baby elephants! It lives in coral reefs and doesn't move once it has settled on the reef. It grows to such a large size because most of its food is made by plantlike algae living in its soft body. The algae give the clam its bright colors and are protected by the clam's hard shell. Clams have no head or gut, but they use a small tube called a siphon to take in water full of oxygen and food. A larger siphon squirts waste material out of the clam's body.

More about giant clams

Average size: 3–6.5 ft (1–2 m) long
Food: sugars and **proteins** made by algae living in shell, and plankton filtered from seawater
Lifespan: up to 100 years
Big fact: Pea crabs sometimes live inside giant clam shells, where they are protected from predators.

The **WHALE SHARK** and the **BASKING SHARK** have the biggest mouths, but they eat the smallest food! These filter-feeders filter plankton from the seawater with their gill rakers.

SPECTACULAR SHARKS

More than 500 different kinds of shark swim through the world's oceans. Discover more about some of the biggest and most spectacular sharks alive today.

The **BASKING SHARK** filters over 396,258 gal (1.5 million l) of water in just one hour through its comblike filters, called gill rakers. It has more than 5000 of these gill rakers.

The **GREAT WHITE SHARK** is the biggest hunting fish in the ocean, and its mouth is big enough to swallow a seal whole. Its biggest, jagged, razor-sharp teeth are up to 2 in (5 cm) long.

The huge **PACIFIC SLEEPER SHARK** feeds on giant Pacific octopuses as well as dead great whales, which sink more than 6500 ft (2000 m) to the bottom of the ocean.

The fastest shark, the **SHORTFIN MAKO**, reaches speeds of up to 30 mph (50 kph). It grow up to 13 ft (4 m) long and has long, pointed teeth, like daggers, to grab slippery fish.

The **BLUNTNOSE SIXGILL SHARK** has a strong body up to 16 ft (5 m) long. Female bluntnose sixgill sharks are big enough to give birth to up to 108 pups at a time!

About half of a **THRESHER SHARK'S** body is taken up by its 10-ft- (3-m-) long tail. It uses this super-long tail to round up shoals of small fish and stun them before it feeds. This big shark has a small mouth, so it can only eat small fish, such as sardines or herring.

The fierce **TIGER SHARK** eats almost anything, from fish, seals, and turtles to dolphins, crocodiles, and other tiger sharks. It even takes bites out of bigger sea creatures, such as whales.

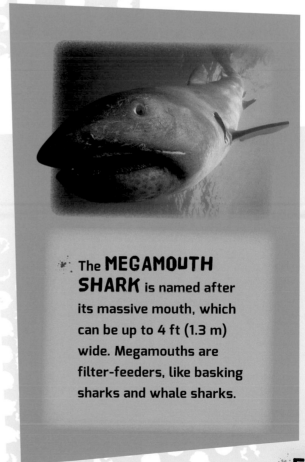

The **MEGAMOUTH SHARK** is named after its massive mouth, which can be up to 4 ft (1.3 m) wide. Megamouths are filter-feeders, like basking sharks and whale sharks.

THE BIG BEASTS QUIZ

Are you an expert on all things big and beastly? Test your knowledge by completing this quiz! When you've answered all of the questions, turn to page 63 to find your score.

 1 **Which is the biggest beast of all time?**
a) African elephant
b) Blue whale
c) Brachiosaurus

 2 **Which is the largest fish alive today?**
a) Basking shark
b) Megalodon shark
c) Whale shark

3 **Which ancient Australian mammal was as big as a rhino?**
a) Giant kangaroo
b) Giant wombat
c) Giant zebra

 4 **What do we call an elephant from the last Ice Age?**
a) Furry tusker
b) Hairy elephant
c) Woolly mammoth

 5 **What is the name of a giant island dragon?**
a) Komodo dragon
b) Lomodo dragon
c) Momodo dragon

 6 **Where does the world's biggest cat live?**
a) Africa
b) India
c) Siberia

 7 **What is the name for a bear's winter rest?**
a) Hibernation
b) Incubation
c) Migration

 8 **Which is the heaviest snake alive today?**
a) Anaconda
b) King cobra
c) Reticulated python

 9 **How long does a newborn elephant take to stand up?**
a) One day
b) One hour
c) One minute

Which are the biggest birds in the world?
a) Emus
b) Ostriches
c) Rheas

 Which moth is as big as a bird?
a) Atlas moth
b) Globe moth
c) Map moth

 In which species of deer do both males and females have antlers?
a) Giant elk
b) Red deer
c) Reindeer (caribou)

 Which chunky safari animal is the third-largest animal on land?
a) African elephant
b) Hippopotamus
c) White rhino

 What do we call an eagle's stick nest?
a) Den
b) Eyrie
c) Lodge

 Which huge seabird may fly 100 miles (160 km) to find breakfast?
a) Giant gannet
b) Great skua
c) Wandering albatross

 Which powerful penguins dive deeper than any other penguin?
a) Emperor penguins
b) Fairy penguins
c) King penguins

 Which deep-sea giant has eyes as big as dinner plates?
a) Goblin shark
b) Giant squid
c) Spectacle sunfish

 What is the favorite food of a great hammerhead shark?
a) Giant octopuses
b) Jellyfish
c) Stingrays

 Which animal has the biggest brain of any animal alive today?
a) Bowhead whale
b) Humpback whale
c) Sperm whale

 How many eggs do gigantic leatherback turtles lay in one clutch?
a) 10
b) 100
c) 1000

GLOSSARY

antler
A twig-like, bony out-growth from the skull of a deer.

bacteria
A large, varied group of very tiny, single-celled living things. Bacteria live in the soil, water, plants, and animals.

blubber
A thick layer of fat under the skin, which helps keep animals warm.

camouflage
The colors and patterns of an animal that help it blend in with its surroundings. This disguise helps it hide from predators or creep up on prey without being seen.

clutch
A number of eggs that are all laid at the same time.

crevice
A narrow crack.

dinosaurs
Prehistoric reptiles, such as Stegosaurus. Dinosaurs once ruled our planet, but died out 65 million years ago.

extinct
Describes a species that has died out and disappeared forever.

fangs
Long, pointed teeth, which may be used to deliver venom, especially in some snakes.

fossilized
The preserved remains of a plant or animal, usually in rock or amber.

gills
The organs that fish and other underwater animals use to take oxygen from the water—a bit like breathing. Gills look like slits on the outside of an animal's body.

hibernating
A kind of rest that some animals take during the long winter months. Animals, such as bears, will stay in their burrows when they are hibernating.

incubation
Sitting on eggs to keep them warm so they will hatch.

invertebrate
An animal without a backbone, for example insects, worms, and spiders.

mammal
A warm-blooded animal that feeds its young on milk.

mammoth
A large, hairy relative of the elephant, which lived in cold places and died out about 10,000 years ago.

mating
When a male and a female animal come together to produce young.

migration
A long journey some animals make each year to a distant place, often to feed and breed, followed by a return trip back.

plankton
Tiny living things that usually just drift in the water.

predator
An animal that hunts and eats other animals for food.

prehistoric
The time before people wrote down any historical records.

prey
An animal that is killed and eaten by another animal.

protein
A nutrient found in food, proteins are required to maintain muscles, bones, blood, and body organs.

pterosaur
A flying reptile, with wings made of skin, which flew in the skies above the dinosaurs.

reptile
An animal with scaly skin and an internal skeleton, which usually lays eggs on land, although some reptiles give birth to live young.

skeleton
The bony framework that supports and protects an animal's body.

species
A group of living things that share similar characteristics and can breed together to produce young.

stamina
The energy to do an activity for a long period of time.

talons
The sharp claws of a bird or animal.

venom
A type of poison that is used in animals' bites or stings to kill prey or as self-defense.

wingspan
The distance from one wingtip to the other wingtip.

QUIZ ANSWERS: 1 = b, 2 = c, 3 = b, 4 = c, 5 = a, 6 = c, 7 = a, 8 = a, 9 = b, 10 = b, 11 = a, 12 = c, 13 = b, 14 = b, 15 = c, 16 = a, 17 = b, 18 = c, 19 = c, 20 = b.

INDEX